YOUR KNOWLEDGE HAS VALUE

- We will publish your bachelor's and master's thesis, essays and papers

- Your own eBook and book - sold worldwide in all relevant shops

- Earn money with each sale

Upload your text at www.GRIN.com
and publish for free

Jenny Ommeln

Interpretation of the poem "Prologue" by Don Paterson

GRIN Verlag

Bibliografische Information der Deutschen Nationalbibliothek:

Die Deutsche Bibliothek verzeichnet diese Publikation in der Deutschen National-
bibliografie; detaillierte bibliografische Daten sind im Internet über http://dnb.d-
nb.de/ abrufbar.

Imprint:

Copyright © 2013 GRIN Verlag GmbH
Druck und Bindung: Books on Demand GmbH, Norderstedt Germany
ISBN: 978-3-656-59783-4

This book at GRIN:

http://www.grin.com/en/e-book/268829/interpretation-of-the-poem-prologue-by-
don-paterson

GRIN - Your knowledge has value

Der GRIN Verlag publiziert seit 1998 wissenschaftliche Arbeiten von Studenten, Hochschullehrern und anderen Akademikern als eBook und gedrucktes Buch. Die Verlagswebsite www.grin.com ist die ideale Plattform zur Veröffentlichung von Hausarbeiten, Abschlussarbeiten, wissenschaftlichen Aufsätzen, Dissertationen und Fachbüchern.

Visit us on the internet:

http://www.grin.com/

http://www.facebook.com/grincom

http://www.twitter.com/grin_com

Goethe-Universität Frankfurt

Seminar: Introduction to Literary Studies

Sommersemester 2013

Interpretation of the poem "Prologue" by Don Paterson

Jenny Ommeln

Major: L1

Semester: 4

The poem "Prologue" by Don Paterson was published in 1997 in his book "God's Gift to Women". Hence, the poem can be classified to the postmodernism, which "is characterized by the self-conscious use of earlier styles and conventions" (Oxford Dictionary, np). The theme of this collection's opening poem is poetry itself and the importance of the lyric persona.

The poem can be roughly divided into an introduction (verse one to eight), a main part (verse nine to 18) and an end (verse 19 to 20). In the introduction the lyric persona rebukes the lyric thou in its behaviour. The main part is a foreshadowing of the upcoming poems of this collection. The poem ends with a demand for praying.

Throughout, the poem is written in couplets and consists of nine sentences that each end with a punctuation. These sentences are mostly structured as enjambments. Therefor not all couplets rhyme, but there is a tendency towards end-rhymes. These enjambments create a continuum in the poem. As a consequence the poem appears to be a speech. The enjambment also establishes a fast rhythm in the first four stanzas, when the lyric persona enumerates the rules of conduct.

Looking closely at the poem's headline, the main aim of the poem becomes obvious. It is called 'Prologue' and functions as the very same thing. A prologue consists of "introductory words addressed to the audience by one of the characters [...] or the author" (Nünning, 193). Instead of the author, the lyric persona addresses the lyric thou and sets the tone for the poems to come. The poem starts with a metaphor when the lyric persona, which appears as an I, states, "a poem is a little church" (v. 1). A church is a visible expression of God's abiding presence. There, people gather to celebrate their faith, to worship their God and to feel his presence. Therefor a poem also connects people. Also, through the lyric persona the author's abiding presence is expressed. Moreover the lyric persona refers to the lyric thou as its congregation. The lyric persona itself is the cantor and thus of a greater spiritual appearance than the lyric thou. This uniqueness is stressed by the following enumeration of the rules of conduct. The introductory part ends with an imperative and the demand to "raise the fucking *tone*" (verse 8). By swearing and writing in italics the lyric persona prepares the addressee for the upcoming part. It becomes clear that the lyric persona will not beautify the truth and that it could get unpleasant. In addition the italics function as a stress to the word and it also refer to the metre that changes from the fifths stanza on.

The lyric persona starts its actual speech that is reminiscent of a sermon. Again, a metaphor is used when the lyric persona announces, "from this holy place of heightened speech, we will join the berry-bus" (v 9-10). This heightened speech refers to the bible. Therefore the collection of poems written in "God's Gift to Women" is of no lesser importance than the texts written in the bible. Moreover the phrase emphasizes that poetry is "a superior instance" (Culler, 69) of literature. In addition the stanza consists of one more metaphor, when the lyric persona announces that the lyric thou will take the "berry-bus in its approach" (v 10). That also relates to the following poems that are each "titled with a specific time and a specific geographic location corresponding to stops on the Scotland's Dundee Newtyle railway" (Donnelly, np). The lyric persona states with the help of a metaphor that the addressee will be going on a journey inward the thoughts and fears of the lyric persona itself (see stanza six). In using irony in stanza six ("where language finds its least prestigious form") the importance of an elevated language is emphasized. It is also a contradictory to the fifths stanza. Again, the imperative is used ("fear not", v 13) to highlight the authority of the lyric persona.

The reference to the train is revisited in the eighth to ninth stanza, where the "coach will limp towards its final stage beyond the snowy graveyard of the page, no one will leave the premises". On the one hand the lyric persona implies a threat that the lyric thou has to read through the whole book on the other hand when looking down on a page, it seems a bit like a snowy graveyard with letters function as tombstones. Moreover in the next two stanzas the lyric persona describes how some of the addressee may feel. In stanza eleven a metaphor is used again to describe the browsing through the book to see how many pages are yet to come.

In the last three stanzas the reference to the church is repeated through metaphors. Roughly summarized verse 25 to 27 mean that the lyric persona will give a lot of input through the upcoming poems and should the addressee not be able to understand the meaning he /she will learn what it means to silently ask other people how they would interpret the read poem. The second part of the 13th stanza consists of a metaphor ("for your roof leaks") and a synecdoche ("and the organ lacks conviction). In Catholicism the roof is the protective cover of faith. Therefor when it leaks the faith will leak as well. As a consequence the metaphor means if poems are not understand well enough the message will not be delivered properly because the addressee will not believe in the message. The synecdoche can be interpreted in the same way. However, it does not refer to the irrational side of believing but rather to the rational side of believing. If a poem is not understood well enough the addressee will not find enough evidences to proof his/hers interpretation.

The poem ends with a relativization of the introductory metaphor. Therefor, a metaphor is used again. The lyric persona wants to express that the poems of the collection are not comprehensive and are of everyday topics. The poem ends with an imperative and a demand to pray (metaphor for starting reading the poems). The last two words are "Oh God" and the poem has no punctuation at the end as if a really prayer is going to start. Summing up the poem consists of a variety of metaphor. It is almost the only rhetorical figure used. Through the tight couplets and the usage of imperatives the lyric persona appears strong. It becomes obvious that the voice of the poem does not belong to the author but to the poem itself.

Bibliography

Culler, Jonathan. *Literary Theory. A very Short Introduction.* Oxford: University Press, 2000. Print.

Donnelly, Timothy. "Nothing, in Other Words: On the Poetry of Don Paterson." cstone.net. Web. 18 June 2013. http://www.cstone.net/~poems/essadonn.htm

Nünning, Vera and Ansgar Nünning. *An Introduction to English and American Literature.* Stuttgart: Klett, 2011. 184-195. Print.

Paterson, Don. "Prologue". *God's Gift to Women.* London: Faber and Faber. 1997

"Potsmodernism." *Oxford Dictionary Online.* Oxford Dictionary. Web. 18 June 2013.